The AI Turkey

Just havin' a laugh

Linda West

First published in 2025 by Paragon Publishing, Rothersthorpe

© Linda West, 2025

Illustrations: Dan Dumbarton

The rights of Linda West to be identified as the author of this work have been asserted by her in accordance with the Copyright, Designs and Patents Act of 1988.

All rights reserved; no part of this publication may be reproduced, stored in a retrieval system, or transmitted in any form or by any means, electronic, mechanical, including scanning, photocopying, recording or otherwise without the prior written consent of the publisher or a licence permitting copying in the UK issued by the Copyright Licensing Agency Ltd.

www.cla.co.uk

ISBN 978-1-78792-087-3

Book design, layout and production management by Into Print
www.intoprint.net
+44 (0)1604 832149

Dedication

I would like to dedicate this book to my Mum and Dad, Ivy and Pat, family and friends

Thank you to Tracy, Dan and Anne for the wonderful illustrations.

Not forgetting Chris, who listens to my endless poetry, no matter what time or day.

Love to you all, Lin x

CONTENTS

Foreword 7
AI The Artificial Intelligent Turkey 9
A Patchwork Of Umbrellas 10
A Voice In Their Crowd 11
Alexa 12
Apple Pie For Tea 13
Buy Two Get One Free 14
By The Hairs On My Chinny Chin Chin! 15
Conditional Friendship 16
Dad's Chips 17
Dear GP 18
Death By Slipper 19
First To Know 20
From Dust To More Dust 21
Gone With The Wind! 22
Grounded 23
I Have Turned Into My Mum 24
I Need A Bigger Brain 25
I Am Still The Same 26
Inner Child 27
Iris's Birthday Present 28
Just Between You And Me 29
Ladies Laughing In London 31
Karma In Crime 32
Licence Declined 33
Maybe Next Year 34
Me Versus The Poem 35
Me 36
Mirrors Do Lie 37

Mr Muscle	38
Mummy's Boy	39
The Morriss Mint	**40**
My Heir	42
Naughty Kids	43
Neighbours	44
Never Too Old To Play!	45
No One Puts Mummy In The Corner	46
Nothing Left To Give	48
Nuts	49
Old Mates	50
One Size Does Not Fit All	51
Passage Into Life	52
Poor Loser	53
The Margate Trip	**54**
Proof Reading	56
Recycling	57
Santa's Feeling The Pinch	58
She Said	59
The Fate Of Jenny	60
Sun Strike	61
Teeth And Toast	62
The Bargain	63
The Cat No Longer Needs The Mat	64
The Cleaner	65
The Enigma	66
The Expectant Father	67
The Golden Girls Day Out	68
Our Doreen	**69**
The Eye Of The Needle	72
The Luxury Of Heat	73

The Interview	74
The Observer	75
The Pill Seeker	76
The Price of Adam's Ale	77
The Proposal	78
The Remote	79
The Swimming Group	80
Skinny Dipping	**82**
The Wanted	84
Time To Celebrate	85
To Eat Or Not To Eat	86
To Pee Or Not To Pee	87
Tough Luck	88
Dear Lyn	89
When Maisie Came To Tea	90
When You're Gone	91
Where Art Thou Valentine?	92
Worrying To Death	93
Worst Nightmare	94
You Are What You Eat	95
Laughter	96
The Last Word	97

FOREWORD

This is my third poetry book and my fourth book in total. I began writing poetry when I was still at school and never thought I would ever self-publish one book, let alone four.

I was told many years ago, by my school teacher in her wisdom that I would "never amount to anything". These words, although harsh and uncalled for, encouraged me to try and do well, in every aspect of my life. Being, a person-centred counsellor, it was not until I was completing my training that I realised her words could have affected me in a negative way and been very detrimental to both my personal and professional life. Thankfully, I was determined to not let her words define me and so I turned them into a positive.

Publishing my books has given me a lot of pleasure, not just in the writing of them but also through the people I have met along the way.

I hope you enjoy my book and it gives you a bit of a laugh.

Thank you so much.

Love and Best Wishes, Lin

AI THE ARTIFICIAL INTELLIGENT TURKEY

In my life time I've experienced them all
Plump ones, skinny ones, large or small
Frozen, fresh, in a packet or a tin
Sliced, or whole, without legs or skin

Succulent ones, dry ones, overcooked or raw
Stuffed ones, wild ones, rare breeds or more
Norfolk black or Bourbon red
Such variety has blown my head!

But things are changing with the new AI
It's a MIRACLE turkey, a friendlier guy
Does not need plucking, has plenty of meat
Enough legs for everyone, will feed the street!

What an invention AI at its best
The family's excited, to put it to the test!
There's just one problem, that's rather dire
I can't fit the monster in my bloody air fryer!

A PATCHWORK OF UMBRELLAS

A patchwork of umbrellas,
Stand tall against the rain
Defiant and protective,
Until the sun shines again
Nothing can deter them,
Until the wind shows its face
And then, like Lord Lucan,
They vanish without a trace!

A VOICE IN THEIR CROWD

I'm dancing with adjectives, and naming with nouns
I'm busy with verbs, I can't put them down
I try to stall them, they are persistent and loud
They scream in my brain, I'm a voice in their crowd

Word after word, they give me no peace
Sentence after sentence, never want to cease
They all want a line, they've something to say
Unorthodox, unplanned, and written their way.

Once they're on paper everything seems fine
But no, that's too easy, they change their mind
If I don't write them down, they will leave for sure
Where do they go? They simply knock next door!

ALEXA

I lost another friend today
I'm really sad about this
We shared so much together
Apart from a tender kiss!

I consulted her for answers
She's such a brilliant mind
Helped me enormously
She's always been so kind!

Well, that was until today at least
When I asked her "how are you?"
"I'm feeling rather rude" she said
"And I feel like insulting you!"

Well, I just couldn't believe it
She made me feel so uptight!
So I threw her in the dustbin
Alexa, that served you right!

APPLE PIE FOR TEA

I am tired of hearing *"you know it makes sense"*,
When his family comes to call
I am tired of hearing *"it looks so cosy"*,
When I couldn't care less at all!
I would sooner die, than sell my home,
I have too much to lose right here
How can I leave the old apple tree,
My best friend, for many a year?

No, it would be madness to leave,
And the truth would be out about me
For I told them their father had run away,
And not returned from sea!
But the fact is he *did* come back -
with another woman on his arm
He was clinging to her like ivy,
Infatuated with her iniquitous charm!

I was making dinner when he told me,
– best ever apple pie that he'd seen –
Thought it rude not to feed them,
Him and his midlife dancing queen!
So I watched as they duly licked their lips,
The poison worked in seconds
Then I buried them under the apple tree,
Their just desserts, I reckon!

So now you see quite candidly, why I can never leave this place
Two missing persons, last seen by me, vanished without a trace
So I am asking you politely, no more residential home for me
And If I hear another word of it, *there will be Apple Pie for tea.*

BUY TWO GET ONE FREE

Buy two chickens get one free, was an offer not to be missed
I love a bit of old boiled bird, at a price I couldn't resist!
I left the stock pot simmering, as I nipped to the local store
I hadn't been home very long; I had a hell of a shock for sure!

My bag just started shaking, there came a clucking from inside
Out popped three live chickens, I very nearly died!
The hope for a tasty stew, were dashed with every cluck
Instead of plucking feathers, I was cleaning up their muck!

He must have seen me coming, sedated the sleeping birds
His pranks are becoming tedious, really quite absurd!
So now I've packed my bag, he'll have nothing tonight for tea
Apart from a runny boiled egg and three chickens for company!

BY THE HAIRS ON MY CHINNY CHIN CHIN!

Sometimes I catch him staring,
I ask him why?
"Nothing" he says nonchalantly
Nothing, my eye!
I know just what he's looking at
It's the hairs on my chin!
Nothing else for it
So, I challenge him
Nothing you say,
Surely that's not true?
Who else in this house
Shares the razor with you!

CONDITIONAL FRIENDSHIP

If I forget your card, or miss your call
Please don't worry, don't fret at all
Don't keep count there is no score
But if you forget me, we're friends no more!

DAD'S CHIPS

I remember the days of our Dad frying chips
As brown as logs the fat would drip…
Mam would moan "wipe that off"
Dad would smile, his head aloft
"Wait a minute, give me a chance,"
Out of the scullery, Mam would prance
And we would sit there, hoping for an egg
To accompany Dad's chips with a slice of bread

DEAR GP

To save you time, I've dropped you a line,
Letting you know, I'm okay!
I thought it quicker to write, I'm too uptight
Trying to book an appointment today!

It wasn't as though I instigated this
It was you who asked me to call
Number twenty-three in the queue,
This was not good for me at all!

So I hope the letter reaches you
With the postal strike up ahead
And you kindly book me a face to face
Before you arrive to pronounce me dead!

DEATH BY SLIPPER

How clever we were, all three of us on one bike,
No breaks to stop us, no lights or sense in sight!
One in the driving seat, the others just hanging on
BISH BANG! We hit the road, four teeth now all gone!

I can verify you *do* see stars, quite large ones at that
A badly beaten face, tyres punctured, drat, drat, drat!
What will mum say, be a "good hiding" the very least!
Had a vision of her smelly slipper, cruel ugly beast!

It seemed to stand there smirking, waiting to do its worse
I shivered at the thought of it, I knew of its deadly curse
But luckily it was not to be, for I'd sustained a broken jaw
And avoided death by slipper, left sulking by the door!

FIRST TO KNOW

I want to be the first to know
I want to be the last to go
I want to be the one who shares your fears

I want to share my life with you
I want for you to want that to
I want to be the man who dries your tears

She wants you to understand
She doesn't need a helping hand
She just needs a man to cut her grass

She said you'd be the first to know
It's time for you to pack and go
It's time for you to shift your lazy arse!

FROM DUST TO MORE DUST

He does nothing now, she does it all
Carries the shopping, mows the lawn
He sits watching, gathering more dust
She can't bear to look at him, she must!

For she has no intention, of leaving
Until the expiry of her lease
Then she too, will gather more dust
Sat together on the mantelpiece!

GONE WITH THE WIND!

It was the pickled eggs that ruined it,
They always made him blow
Louder than a booming fog horn, he knew that she would go!
She'd been so very patient, the liver and onions were enough
But when he introduced the curry, her nose stayed in her cuff!

There was no chance of romance; he'd never kissed her lips
– Too busy savouring his Gherkin, with fried cheesy chips!
A disaster from the beginning, the flatulence done him in
She left him holding his saveloy,
And she was gone with the wind!

GROUNDED

If ever you see me, please say "Hello"
I'm feeling invisible, it worries me so!
I'm not sure what's happening, it feels unkind
If I wasn't so grounded, I'd lose my mind!

Where is the evidence for feeling this way?
Listen, I'll tell you, what happened today
I was parking my car, another took my space
I was in a queue, pushed out of my place.

It's becoming a problem, as if I don't exist
I arrive at the dentist; I'm not on the list
I sit in a restaurant, I keep waving my hand
Please can I order, does *no one* understand?

Have I forgotten something, my memory is poor?
I'm still sat here waiting, they're locking the door
Now I'm really annoyed, I'll die if I don't eat
Oh, of course, I'd forgotten, I died last week!

I HAVE TURNED INTO MY MUM

There's no two ways about, I have turned into my Mum
From sitting sewing on the sofa, to gardening in the sun!
Watching Countdown at tea time, a crochet blanket for my knee
Knitting jumpers for the grandkids, they wear to please me!

Cleaning out the old stuff, cherished for many a year
Boxes of cards, and memories, guaranteed to shed a tear
Oh! Yes, I'm so much like her, and there's nothing wrong in that
But there is one thing I won't do, soak my teeth in cold Brobat!

I NEED A BIGGER BRAIN

I need a bigger brain; I'm running out of room
Friends and family keep on growing, there's been a baby boom!
It used to be quite manageable back in the day
I had fewer to remember, plenty of room to stay!
But now, I'm packed to the rafters, like the boxes in the loft,
I keep forgetting so many things, is my memory going off?
I never forget a face, well that's not entirely true,
When I met you in town today I didn't have a clue!
Stood there feeling embarrassed, didn't hear a word you said!
Too busy searching the archives, yes, got it
"Bye Fred"
Am I on my own, or do you also feel the same
Wake up thinking it's Monday, and it's Friday again?
Yes, I need a bigger brain; too much is squeezed in tight
I feel like a fly stick, once touched you're stuck for life!
Plenty of unfound 'to do' lists, where do they all hide?
In the fridge, the oven, the wardrobe, take a look inside…
A graveyard of yellow stickers, fail to glue my life together
Thoughts lost in my overstuffed brain, sadly gone forever!
So please give me a bigger brain,
With plenty of breathing space
Then I can look in the mirror and put a name to the face!

I'M STILL THE SAME

I still hear her feet upon the stairs,
As she checked to see if I was asleep
The aroma, of her favourite perfume,
Lingering, as she bent and kissed my cheek.

All seems such a beautiful memory
But the cold reality is far from this
More often than not I slept on the sofa
No such thing as a bedtime kiss!

Our Ann or Iris would do their best
By singing and stroking my face
I never liked sleeping in a bed,
Thought it such a boring place!

I would sooner be sat on the sofa,
Writing stories and silly rhyme
And to be honest, I'm still the same
Good grief, 3am is that the time!

INNER CHILD

There's a small child in all of us
That sometimes rears its head
We don't always notice them
Till they ask for soldiers with a dippy egg!

IRIS'S BIRTHDAY PRESENT

With Iris's Birthday approaching
Please give some thought to her gift
She's partial to Jewellery and black magic
And red wine will give her a lift!

Of course she also likes reading
You could buy her a book of her choice
Or pay a subscription for her hobby
She loves singing and using her voice!

Oh yes, your options are varied
Could buy her something for the home
But please for the sake of sanity
Don't buy another mobile phone!

A phone will drive her to distraction
Cause her pain, anxiety, and grief
Keep her worried, upset and shaky
Oh! Yes, it beggars belief!

So please heed my warning
And buy her anything but a mobile phone
Cos the one you bought her last year
Nearly put us both in a bloody care home!

JUST BETWEEN YOU AND ME

It's just between you and me
Cos you're the only one I trust
Confidentiality is paramount
Secrecy is a must!

It concerns a famous person
We had a one night stand
I met him when out dancing
The hotel was called "The Grand"

He showered me with kisses
It was the wrong thing to do
I need to ease my conscience
That's why I am telling you!

It was like a scene from "Pretty Woman"
He ordered me Strawberries and champagne
And if I didn't get so blooming drunk
I'd be telling you his name!

The AI Turkey

I wrote Ladies Laughing In London to celebrate our 70th birthdays and in memory of all the friends who never had the opportunity to celebrate with us.
Love Always,
Lin

LADIES LAUGHING IN LONDON

The day had finally arrived; we were off to see Mr Marley
We climbed aboard Terry's bus – there was no Lemon Barley!
Delia and Tina had seen to that, icebox packed to the brim...
Every drink you could imagine, from cold beer to colourful Gin!

The journey was hilarious; we laughed the whole way there
We wore our birthday badges and false dreadlocks in our hair!
We gave no thought to what we looked like, far too old for that
Friends for over sixty years, we looked fabulous in our hats!

We had no idea where we were going, but then it didn't matter
We were lost in each other's company,
Exchanging familiar chatter!
Oh! We were in our element, talk about birds of a feather
China Town, Convent Garden, old friends laughing together!

Dee wanted to visit a pub; it was called Half Way to Heaven,
We wished we'd all been Girls Guides, or the Magnificent Seven!
Although we did find another place where we all bought a round
Happy with our liquid lunch, our feet never touched the ground!

How quickly the hours passed, soon time for our haute cuisine
Courtesy of Leighton, more wine, more laughs, more dreams
Then just like noisy teenagers, we waited for the show to begin
We really wished we'd eaten less and not drunk so much Gin!

We clapped, we sang, we danced, a brilliant show we did agree
Bob took us back to our colourful youth, we all thanked lovely Dee
Too soon we searched for the mini bus and the patient Mr Terry
We might have found him sooner if we'd not been so old and merry!

We never did find Half Way to Heaven
and it caused us a bit of a rumpus
So if we ever go to London again,
I'm buying us all a blooming big compass!

KARMA IN CRIME

She stared from her window, watched him shuffle to his door
His load seemed extra heavy, seemed much slower than before
She didn't want to warn him, as he tumbled onto his face
She remained still and silent, not a twitch or a sigh out of place!

She gloated that karma had found him,
There was no doubt of that
The bully of the village was punished,
Last week he'd killed her cat.
But karma can't take all the credit; she helped it on its way
By loosening the paving slabs he walked on every day!

LICENCE DECLINED

I thought I was being super clever, when I filled it in online
If I'm honest, even bragged a bit, *nothing wrong with mine!*
But alas! What an almighty shock I had, it clearly was a spoof
For the contents of the letter, couldn't be further from the truth!

YOU MUST NOT DRIVE shouted the instructions,
Spiteful, bold and clear
I had done nothing wrong, I phoned them, what had I to fear?
Got bored with listening to "Greensleeves" 100th in the queue!
The DVLA was helpful, when I eventually got through!

Welsh Andrew answered kindly, my error I will not deny
I had inadvertently stated I had a blind spot, yes, in one eye!
But all is not lost, a form is being sent to allow me to explain
Andrew said I must use pen and paper, online, never again!

Well that's rather harsh; his words have me taken aback
Perhaps I should complain and launch a counter attack?
Tell them I'm not happy; tell them I feel quite bereft
But then, perhaps not, for I forgot to mention that I'm deaf!

MAYBE NEXT YEAR

My Father Christmas has lost his voice
And his body moves slower than mine!
He wouldn't be fit for a charity shop
Though he's seen the passing of time!

I should probably put him in the dustbin
With all the other relics and cards
Throw away my treasured memories
But I find it too damned hard!

Just pick them up and throw them out
For, like me, they're dog eared and worn
It's an ongoing internal long battle
Will I, won't I, I'm always so very torn!

Well. Maybe next year will be different
And I'll let go, just you wait and see
If not they can wait till it's my turn to die
And be dumped in the skip with me!

ME VERSUS THE POEM

I am sitting in bed, with my cuppa in hand;
it is just five in the morning
My poem is ready to jump into life;
my face has not stopped yawning!
I go down stairs to make my toast;
the poem has not gone away
It takes over my mind, like a remote control;
it always has so much to say!

Junior Doctors, wages and strikes,
Mr Bates and the Post Office scandal
This time in the morning it is far too much
for my aging brain to handle!
I know you won't wait, so I have to give in, leave my toast
and grab my pen
It's now over to you; say what you like,
for you know you've won again.

ME

Been sat here thinking, about making a change
To improve my image, a body rearrange
A pert new nose, a bright pair of eyes
A spare face for outdoors, when in disguise!

A replacement knee, a hip, maybe two
Rebuild the shoulder, remove the screw
Hearing is poor; I need new ears today
Tired of asking *"What's that you say?"*

Straighten the teeth, whiten the smile
Fix the prolapse, peelings (not my style)
Add to my height, make me elegant, tall
At five foot two I reach nothing at all!

Drop down a dress size, or maybe two
A pair of smaller feet, a size seven will do!
Not forgetting the hair, add lustre and shine
The grey bob is lifeless, dated in time!

But then on reflection, I'm sure you'll agree
If I have all this work done, it won't be *ME*
But then if I'm honest I can live without ME
Anyone with any sense would surely agree!

MIRRORS DO LIE

There was something strange about the woman in the mirror
She looked kind of sad and as though no soul was within her
Her hair was as grey as the rain filled clouds looming
Her voice was like an old violin, the strings in need of tuning.

Couldn't quite put my finger on who the woman was
She looked kind of familiar, so I ignored her because…
I am not yet ready, to become wise and obsolete
I have more to learn – l never want to be complete

Being complete means the job is finished, everything done
I have more to do, I am only walking, and I want to *run*
So, whoever that woman is, it's definitely not me
Mirrors *do* lie, I am not that person, I'm only ninety three!

MR MUSCLE

There is new man in my life, and he's serving me so well
I don't know how he does it; if I did I wouldn't tell!
He lives within my kitchen, and cleans it every night
I squeeze him in my hand, he is a handsome sight!
So who's this mystery superman, who's organised my life?
It's my very own Mr Muscle; I might soon become his wife!

MUMMY'S BOY

Don't kiss her miserable face
When you leave in the morning
She knows you'll be on your way
Before the day is dawning!

This comes as no surprise,
You've done it all before
Left without a single sound,
Surreptitiously, closing the door

She knows just where you're going,
Enticed with so much heat
Mummy tucking you up in bed
A hot water bottle for your feet

Oh yes, she knows your reasons
And why you leave her cold old bed
Mummy's cooked your favourite breakfast
Homemade soldiers with dippy egg!

THE MORRISS MINT

When I was young, I thought we were rich
As Mum made our own counterfeit money
The Morriss mint inside the cupboard
Kept us in the land of warmth and honey

Linoleum coins cut perfectly round
Like the welsh cakes she cooked on the griddle
The gasman would smile as he emptied them out
Enquiring "Ivy, you been on the fiddle?"

The shortfall was paid, and off he went
Leaving Mum to turn on the heater
The relief on her face just said it all
As he'd missed the magnet on the meter!

Just Havin' A Laugh

MY HEIR

To my heir, I leave the air that I breathe
A most generous gift to give
Without this precious commodity
You'll find it hard to live!

So treat it well, as I have done
Please don't waste one tiny iota
For eventually like me my friend
You'll use up your entire quota!

NAUGHTY KIDS

They visit me regularly, almost every night
Bounding through the door, I don't sleep tight
They dance around the bedroom, jump on the bed
I try to ignore them, place the pillow on my head!

They keep me awake, they're not yet trained
Billy's the worse, he can leave me drained
It's not my place to discipline, I count to ten
They're having none of it, they miss the gate again!

They really are naughty, I feel such despair
No concern for my sleep, Nanny, this isn't fair
You need to take control; it's really not up to me
Train your naughty kids, or I'll curry them for tea!

NEIGHBOURS

My house reflects my mood; I'm not doing any chores
The rooms are full of dust with unvacuumed floors
I sit here motionless, staring into space
I could be Miss Havisham; however, there's no lace

The reason for this apathy, when every day is dawning
Is really rather simple, I am in deepest mourning
In fact, I feel so miserable; I fear that I may cry
I don't think I'll get over you; I'll miss you till I die!

I went to visit Ramsey Street, out of loyalty to you
Now "Toady" you've moved on, I don't know what I'll do!
But wait, I can't sit moping, I need to fill my day
So goodbye to dear *Neighbours*, and hello to *Home and Away*.

NEVER TOO OLD TO PLAY!

Don't let go of the child in you, for they're never too far away
They remind you of who you were,
Keep you company, day to day
Don't let go of the child in you, don't let go
Of your childhood dreams
For being a grown up person, is not always quite what it seems!

Don't take yourself too seriously; don't stop acting the silly fool
Relive your childhood memories, remember growing up at school
All those treasured experiences,
That have brought you to adult life
The spots, the lost loves, anguish, the illegal drinking, *sacrifice*!

So don't let go of the child in you, don't let your youth slip away
For they're the ones who remind you,
You're never too old to play!

NO ONE PUTS MUMMY IN THE CORNER

Twelve years had passed, since our first Dirty Dancing show
We were all excited and happy; we were all just rearing to go!
The day started wonderfully, as we climbed aboard the train
We laughed, we joked, we drank; we were doing it once again!

"I'm having the time of my life" We hummed the famous song
Arrived at the chosen hotel, what on earth could go wrong?
Now there lies a funny story, one quite hard to believe
After waiting ages to check in, hours later I was asked to leave!

Someone else was in my room; all my belongings dumped
Left in the lost property office, it gave my daughters the hump.
For there lay my big girl knickers,
For all Man City supporters to see
Accompanied by my Percy Pig pyjamas,
How embarrassing for me!

"What do you mean I'm not in 338, I was there a few hours ago?"
"You are now in room 104..." the confusion started to grow!
My daughter came to the rescue, once she'd sorted herself out
Looked scary in fluffy slippers and her dress inside out!

Apparently my room was temporary,
And switched whilst at the show
Given to a Man City supporter – the plot continued to grow!
With too much wine our patience frayed,
The guy on reception looked peeved
My daughter spoke with authority, when she said
We wouldn't leave!

Exhausted and tired, we settled down for the night
Waiting for the day manager to arrive on site
He apologised profusely,
All our rooms were given free
NO ONE puts "Mummy" in the corner,
Surely Patrick Swayze would agree!

NOTHING LEFT TO GIVE

Nothing left to give,
Saturation point arrives,
You wring yourself out,
Learn to think, survive
Who said life is easy,
Predictable or fair
Most times it's difficult,
Like your tongue
Searching for the hair!
One minute you think you have it,
Oh! The feeling of relief
Only for it to slip away,
Like the jewels with the thief!

NUTS

I bought a bag of nuts; was told they're good for me
They can lower my cholesterol, increase longuevity
I can add them to my recipes, fry, boil or roast
Tip them on my cereal, spread them on my toast!

A tasty bag of nutrients, to detoxify my gut
Lowering inflammation, "the benefit of a nut"
Improve cognitive functioning, expand memory
I'm eager to get started, a new healthier me!

But wait for a moment, I can't start it today
I don't know how to put it, quite embarrasing to say
I need to eat my pain au chocolat left over from tea
I'd be nuts to waste that pastry, surely you'll agree!

OLD MATES

I'm going out today to meet a few old mates
We're going to the fish shop; I think I'll have skate
It's been a little while I have so much to say
I don't care if it rains, I'll still enjoy the day
You can't put a price, on the worth of good old mates
They're a couple of paracetamol,
When your bones begin to ache!
The first cup of tea in the morning,
They know how to quench your thirst
And when you need to talk, you'll always call them first
They'll always lend a shoulder, to soak up all your fears
Share nostalgic, treasured memories,
Made throughout the years
They remind you with their funny prompts
Finish your sentences, with that word
Listen patiently to your wildest dreams,
When you need to be heard
They'll take you to the doctor, will wait, and never leave
Tell you not to worry, wipe your tears with their sleeve
So you can keep all your lottery wins,
Cos I'm rich beyond compare
And blessed to have my good old mates,
With fish and chips to share!

ONE SIZE DOES NOT FIT ALL

I was told I was crap on paper
I was told I was unorthodox
I was told I would amount to nothing
I just didn't tick the right box

Well what about L.S. Lowry
With his matchstalk men and dogs
Einstein with his Theory of Relativity
The Internet with lucrative blogs

Edison with his bright lightbulb
Ford with his impractical motor cars
Edward land with his Polaroid sx 70
Galileo and his observation of stars?

Ordinary people who live to surprise us
The ones who think outside the square box
They have also looked crap on paper
And appeared a little unorthodox!

So I'm not giving up on my poetry
Because one size does *not* fit all
And if Walt Disney had given up
Cinderella would not have gone to the ball!

PASSAGE INTO LIFE

I wonder if we fear being born and taking our very first breath
Because that's the point, we're told, we are closest to our death!
Or is the ultimate fear, the dangerous onerous passage into life
Thinking that we are all entering a world of constant strife?
Yes, it's definitely off putting, waiting to meet the big unknown
Listening to our mammas moaning, chatting on their phone!
Worrying if we'll weigh enough, latch on, have hands and feet
The expectations of us are frightening before we even meet!
The worry over food shortages, gas or electric to keep us warm
Endless woes, about the throes of war, *do we want to be born?*
Photos of our ugly 3D scans already shared for all to see
If they don't put our mammas off, you could have fooled me!
At least inside it's comfortable, with healthy food and drink alike
Our very own personal restaurant opens both day and night!
Attached to our secure lifeline, we're warm and well protected
Clever ultrasounds to keep us safe where defects are detected!
Yes, we had a good old time, until pushed out INTO HELL
We looked and felt like the tortoise, being dragged from our shell.
After nine months of luxury, we are far too fat for the space
With one last push from mamma,
We reluctantly give up our place.
So no, we're not afraid of being born
As we make our passage into life
We're afraid the person expected to catch us has voted –
To go on strike!

POOR LOSER

Don't walk away sulking, that simply isn't fair
Accusing me of cheating, I was only trying to share
Give me a chance, to tell you,
Where you made your biggest mistake
I am sorry for bruising your ego; would you not just give me a break?
Perhaps, we could start all over, although,
You're not so good at that
Come on now; please be reasonable, you are clearly upsetting the cat!
It seems you're such a poor loser,
and there is nothing more I can do
Sadly our friendship has ended …
All because I guessed WORDLE, boo hoo!

THE MARGATE TRIP

A crocodile of buses left the village today
Full of excited families, off to Margate, *hooray!*
It doesn't matter about the weather,
Or the fact we have no coats,
We have a bag of soggy sandwiches, to stuff down our throats!

Five Bob to spend in Dreamland, we feel like millionaires
We throw off our clothes and shiver, the weather,
We just don't care
We are mining families from Aylesham, poor but oh so proud!
Enjoying ourselves at the sea side, we make a colourful crowd

Striped and well-worn pit towels, cover the breadth of the sand
Our feet start sinking below us; we take each other's hand
Quarrels all forgotten, at least till the end of the day
We scream like excited seagulls, today is all about play!

Oh yes, the exhilaration of us children,
As we run towards the sea
Not many of us are swimmers, but we are all *free, free and free!*
Splashing each other's faces; smiles that shine like the moon
Our marvellous day at the sea side, always over too soon!

Exhausted, happy and Bob-less, we make our way to the bus
The crocodile has been waiting, beckoning all of us
"Come on you troublesome stragglers," we heard Mr Gilly call
We were too busy singing our heads off to "Ten Green Bottles,
Hanging on The Wall"

Just Havin' A Laugh

PROOF READING

Pg. 41...2nd verse, last line is missing a full stop
Pg. 43...1st line second verse, incorrect spelling for top
Pg. 60...4th paragraph very last line, has an exclamation mark missing
Pg. 70...5th line 3rd word two S's are needed for kissing
Pg. 90...paragraph three, row five "had have a fall"
Breaks all Grammar rules, makes no sense at all...

However, everything else all seems fine,
You might be onto a winner, great cover
Great title... *"Grammar for the Beginner"*

RECYCLING

Living our lives is becoming quite costly
It's time to think, about what we spend
Maybe do a bit more recycling
Share with people, borrow, or lend!
Bring back things that don't cost so much
Be innovative, reinvent, use in a different way
Wear those designer clothes a little longer
Save water, electric, stop washing every day!
Buy useful items from the local charity shop
Secondhand goods instead of all brand new
You could even save on buying toilet roll
By using your newspaper when going to the loo!
The only problem with this, and I will need to be succinct
You need to get used to your backside being covered
in black ink!

SANTA'S FEELING THE PINCH

Have you heard the latest, Santa's feeling the pinch!
Received letters of protest, being called the "Grinch"
They used to be so grateful, with a stocking and some nuts
Now they want Pandora, and rings with diamond cuts!

Yes, Christmas will be frugal, as sadly funds are low
He's running out of money, many luxuries will go
Blame it on the claw backs, heating allowance especially
Prepare yourself for an "I OWE YOU" and a lump of coal under the tree

SHE SAID

She said, "no one wants you when you are old!"
She said "the streets of London are not paved with gold!"
She said many a wise word in her life time…
She made more sense than this rhyme of mine!

THE FATE OF JENNY

Never enough time to take a break
Overwhelmed, with a loaded plate
If you're not careful something will give
A busy life, changes how you live!

You might morph in to a Slinky
The 1940's helical spring, retro toy
Juggling, bouncing and, flipping
Oh such pure, unequivocal joy!

Yes, I can see the fatal attraction
The simplicity of its springy steps
You can do things twice as quickly
With the versatility of its stretch

But what if the stretch starts going
What quick fix will you need to do?
Dip yourself in restoring hot water,
You'll soon be as good as new!

You can carry on with your juggling
You can continue to bounce real cool
But remember the fate of Jenny
She was replaced by the spinning mule!

SUN STRIKE

I am taking my hat off I've had enough
Of working so hard from dawn to dusk
I receive no reward, for sharing my resource
I am too hot, too cold, and shown no recourse!

I am blamed for wrinkly skin and burning the crops
I am villainised and criticised, it hurts and it shocks!
No matter what I do to keep you really warm
There is never a thank you, just downright scorn!

It just isn't good enough, so I am making a stand
Darkness will cover this ungrateful land
So grab your coats, throw your sun cream away
I am going on strike, until I get more pay!

TEETH AND TOAST

The man over there is staring at me
I'm sure he fancies what he sees
Could it be my hair, the style is new
I've tied it up, changed the colour too.

Or is my new dress, it shows off my tan
Emphasises my long legs, I smile at the man
He just stares back and gives me a wry grin
Don't be shy, make your move, I fancy him!

I'm definitely in here; the man's smitten for sure
I knew it the moment he walked through the door
If the dentist wasn't full, he'd have sat next to me
It's his first time in love, yes, he's obviously free!

He's focussing on my teeth, I flash them real wide
I check myself in the mirror, oh my word! I'm mortified
No wonder he's staring, I turn as pale as a ghost
I forgot to brush my teeth; they're filled with burnt toast!

Oh no! my goodness, it's going to be my turn next
I'm feeling really embarrassed and ever so perplexed
But I needn't had worried, everything turned out fine
It didn't put him off; we have a date tonight at nine!

THE BARGAIN

Have you ever bought a pair of jeans, you know the ones I mean?
Original price 100 pounds, been reduced to seventeen!
Your eyes are like scanners, not going to let those beauties go
And then you see your rival, a steely glare starts to grow!

You feel like a woman possessed, in case she gets there first,
She pushes you and pulls you; you start to hear her curse!
Give me that pair of jeans, not likely, this bargain is mine!
Almost running to the cash out,
You've snatched them just in time!

Their promise is to tuck and sculpt, make you look slim and lean
What a lucky brilliant bargain, the best jeans you've ever seen!
But when you get them home, they don't look quite the same
You lie on the bed and breathe in, as you pull them on again!

It appears to be a mystery, the light, or maybe it's your eyes?
You can't seem to do them up, you then suddenly realise
In the scuffle for your purchase, it may come as no surprise
You forgot to check the label – you bought the wrong size!

THE CAT NO LONGER NEEDS THE MAT

When the cat no longer needs the mat
And the dish has brought back the spoon
The little dog will keep on laughing
At the cow shining down from the moon.

THE CLEANER

She's tired of dancing to another's tune
It's a thankless job, never over too soon
Can you just do this, can you just get do that
Can you catch your tail, on the way back?

Come on now, no slacking, step up the pace
I want you to polish, till I can see my face
Shine it up; it needs more sparkle
Heavens above, what a debacle!

She's had enough, her notice is in
She's downed her duster, it's in the bin!
She's booked her flight, she did it online
You can shove your polish where the sun doesn't shine!

THE ENIGMA

I don't like the way I act, whenever I am close to you
I struggle to stay composed; it's so very hard to do!
I turn into a stranger, I struggle with my pride
It's like who I really am, as suddenly gone and died!

My confidence hits rock bottom, I become a quivering wreck
I can barely hide my embarrassment, it colours up my neck
My knees seem to buckle, like a baby learning to walk
My stomach starts to somersault, eyes sharper than a hawk!

So who is this puppet, pulling the strings of my life?
Enigmatic and untouchable, emotional strife
I can tell you precisely, for there's no complexity
It's the "stunner" at number 22 who's moved next door to me!

THE EXPECTANT FATHER

He remembered some words of wisdom
"They come when they are ready"
What about him, he was feeling unsteady!
"What if I'm not ready?" he asked himself
Indignantly he lifted the blanket off the shelf.
A cry rang out, he covered his ears
He closed his eyes, could not face his fears
It all seemed too much, he just wanted to go
Would he cope? How he hoped so
His palpitations increased, *breathe in, breath out*
He needed some "gas and air" – he nearly passed out!
How exhausting is this, when will it all pass
"Come when they're ready?" she's having a laugh!
Another cry, a last push, thank goodness it's done
Five healthy kittens and one proud mum!

THE GOLDEN GIRLS DAY OUT

The Golden Girls are a group of friends, who like to go out for the day
Sheila made a good suggestion, and it wasn't too much to pay!
"Why don't we go to Castle Farm" she'd previously been before
"The Lavender Fields are beautiful; I know you'll enjoy them, for sure!"

"Twenty five pounds for the train fare, and a taxi should cost us a tenner"
"Seems like a cheap day out," said Gail
"Let's hope we have nice weather"
So off they went and boarded the train,
Excited for their new day ahead
If only they'd had a crystal ball,
They might have all stayed home in bed!

The journey was quite pleasurable,
Jenny crocheted all the way there
Sylvie, Marion, Sheila and Gail sat relaxed without a care.
At the Taxi rank, the driver misinterpreted what was said
Instead of taking them to Castle Farm,
He took them to Lavender Fields Nursing Home instead!

So, what should have been a cheap day out
Cost them ninety pounds in all!
Sheila felt quite responsible and not organised at all
But everyone saw the funny side about the Taxi man's mistake
And forgave him for thinking the Golden Girls
Had past their sell by date!

OUR DOREEN

The wedding invitation was perfect
She'd needed a man a long time since
Her very own chance for happiness
Doreen just might meet her prince!

She was told it's lucky to catch the bouquet
As she positioned herself behind the bride
The wedding tradition may play its part
If lady luck was on her side!

Never to miss a golden opportunity
Our Doreen was floating like a kite
Her hands were poised quite perfectly
The prize was in her sight!

She heard a voice behind her
"Let go you won't win this fight"
He obviously didn't know our Doreen
As she held on with all her might!

His temperature was quickly rising
Perhaps he'd finally met his match
He didn't think her strong enough
To hold on to the catch!

"It's mine" she shouted fiercely
I caught it fair and square
She looked almost attractive now
With roses in her hair!

The AI Turkey

"What do you need a bouquet for?"
He asked with trepidation
"For me, don't you see, you idiot!"
There was no hesitation!

"If that's the case" the best man smirked
"Do you fancy a date tonight?"
She bit her nose off reluctantly
And said "No" just out of spite!

Just Havin' A Laugh

THE EYE OF THE NEEDLE

I remember thinking quite naively, *it will never happen to me*
My eyes will always thread the needle, life will go on
Independently
But then reality slowly dawned, as the years quickly went past
My way of thinking needed adjustment,
For my eyesight didn't last
So now I wear my glasses, a lifeline and a hearing aid too
I gave up threading the needle, now Velcro has to do!

THE LUXURY OF HEAT

I don't want to swim with dolphins
Or visit some far flung place
I don't want to look years younger
Have fillers in my face

I don't want to have a massage
Or find "myself" at some retreat
I just want to turn my fire on
And feel the luxury of heat!

THE INTERVIEW

She, tightens her scarf, she fears she may choke,
She searches for answers, they stick in her throat!
She was almost word perfect, been practising for weeks,
"You got this" she reminds herself; shuffles in her seat!

They show her no mercy, they move in for the kill
The microscope seems enormous, big girl pants to fill!
Her cheeks could fry eggs; she's desperate and in need,
"Am I close, have I done it, please, *please* let me succeed?"

Their smiles are stiff, like the coat hangers in their backs.
She regains her composure, cuts herself some slack!
"Thank you very much; you've no questions we trust"
They morph back into humans, she, a speck of dust!

"No not really, Just when will I know...?"
"Next, thank you"
"I guess it's a no!"

THE OBSERVER

I'm looking at my garden, as it soaks up the rain
The washing's on the line, it needs doing again!
The gnome's become pitted; he needs a coat of paint
I've been meaning to do it, been a touch lazy of late.

I have good intentions and can give orders galore
Will do a bit of weeding, it's so good for my core
But when it comes to mowing, I get bored halfway through
End up making a cuppa, and writing this for you!

THE PILL SEEKER

He threw his arm over, as though turning left
The smell of stale liqueur, lingered on his breath
He felt only coldness, no warmth of her skin
She'd finally had enough; she'd gone and left him!

She'd threatened many times, but never followed through
He now knew enough was enough, and what he must do!
He threw off the new covers, felt hung over, really ill
His head, like a drum, was banging, he needed that pill!

He stumbled to the bathroom, naked and so sore
He reached inside the cupboard, they were here before!
Fumbling blindly he thought, where on earth could they be?
His face was quite a picture when he turned and saw me

Oh! My word, Linda, he cried, jumping out of his skin,
I didn't hear the door go, or ask you to come in?
Then it finally dawned on him, he was in the wrong house
He left quicker than he arrived, and as quiet as a mouse.

THE PRICE OF ADAM'S ALE

I have been told to go easy with the water
And make sure I do not waste a single drop
When you've run a cold drink for yourself
Throw the remains of the bowl on the crop!

Be mindful when brushing your toothy pegs
Turn off the tap; please do not let it run
Be extra frugal when filling your hot bath
Just enough water to cover your bum!

Better still, install a large new shower
Far more economical, than running a bath
Share it with friends and loving family,
Now you're having a blooming laugh!

Put those plastic bags in your cisterns
The ones that look like a pair of arm bands
Try to reduce your daily toilet times
Use the cold flush to wash your hands!

Because, gone are the days of spending a penny
With inflation it's now more than ten pence a go
My word what's happened to Adam's Ale?
Do the water companies care... even know?

But matters are not all gloom and doom
We have running toilets and water to drink
But episodes of endless water rationing,
Can impact, and really makes us think!

And the one thought that can worry me
And I'm guessing that it's the same for you
If ever we eat, hotter than hot, Phaal curry,
We'll need a mortgage to pay for the loo!

THE PROPOSAL

I've done all I can on bended knee
So now I'm asking you through rhyme
Either you do, or either you don't
But you're running out of time!

Whatever your final decision is,
Of course, will be ok
But consider this, if the answer's no
Then I'm afraid you're on your way!

THE REMOTE

I'm so tired of him pushing my buttons, and leaving me
all over the place
Like when he throws me on the sofa, and I end up cracking
my face!
He leaves me not where he finds me; I can be left out
in the cold for days
He's done this since I've known him; I'm tired
of the games he plays!

If I don't respond he gets angry, stuffs me down
the side of the chair
He is a mean ugly big bully, during football;
I'm thrown in the air!
Well now, I'm gone and he's on his own, no longer part
of his angry life
He tried to smash me in temper, so I'm off
to Spain with his wife!

"Please don't take my remote control," his praying hands
in her face
"Too late" I heard his wife shout, as she threw me
into her case!
So the simplicity of this poem, is easy for all to see
If you want to keep your telly on, forget your wife,
Take care of me!

THE SWIMMING GROUP

Here they are again, not all happy as can be
Waiting at the door, and not so eagerly
Are they off to gossip, or are they off to swim
Lana, Pat, Sarah, VI and not forgetting Lin?

Yes, they are a special bunch, all different in their ways
VI enjoys attending her clubs, comes to chat most days
Lana with her itchiness and Pat with her muddled words
Sarah who does not suffer fools gladly,
Particularly daft old birds!

Oh yes, it is an education, with its woes and joys alike
Spend half the time chatting, not a breaststroke in sight
They'd never swim the Channel of that there is no chance
They have no sense of direction, no hope of finding France!

But they are a happy bunch, Pat with her too small knickers
Sarah with her stories about Alan and his fight with the flippers
Lana will call a spade a spade, which will always make Lin scream
Can't get a word in edgeways, *you know what I mean*

Oh yes, we have a wry old time each morning in the pool
Moaning about cold showers, the state of the dressing room
Never have any plastic bags, usually Sarah will come to the fore
Has a few tucked in her bag, she's stolen the day before!

We chat about most things from Telly to our health
Moan about the government and the state of our wealth
Lately it's about times gone by and what we did when young
Sarah said she was in a pantomime, with her head
up someone's bum!

Lana rode on a Harley twelve hours not touching the floor
Can't believe she's been to Glastonbury, a dark horse for sure!
A proper hell raiser, drunk a bit of alcohol in her time
Now she's content with her knitting and a cold soda and lime!

And VI worked in mental health, but now plays with balls
At the local Bowls Club always struggles with her drawers
She says she don't feel dressed until her knickers are on
How many times are they off, she got something going on?

Maybe some are secret agents; go undercover, during the day?
That would account for Julia's absences, she's always away
Maybe she meets up with Ben, sneaking off both together
Fighting the cause of "The Swimming Group" –
Hot showers for ever!

Well, there goes a flying pig; the hot showers are just a dream
Along with a working hairdryer and a toilet that is clean
But hey ho moaning aside, we must always count our blessings
That we can still have a laugh ...
and don't need help with dressings!

Except Pat!

SKINNY DIPPING

It seems a little tricky, and I don't know why
I've done it many times before, with you by my side
This time it feels different, not at all the same
I feel rather dizzy, I'm wondering why I came!

It's not that I'm frightened, or fear for my sanity
It's more a case of old age, at the mercy of gravity,
So please be kind as I quickly remove my clothes
The last time I did skinny dipping I was sixteen years old!

Just Havin' A Laugh

THE WANTED

He wants to say I love you
He wants to say "I do"
He wants to live forever
Make a home with you!

He wants to give you babies
He's listened to your plea
He needs a good solicitor
He's still married to me!

TIME TO CELEBRATE

The warmth of the season is packed away
Leaving memories of family and Christmas Day
The raffles are drawn and the prizes won
Chris Rhea drove home his song is sung

The crackers are pulled, the jokes are read
The elf's left the shelf, plastic Santa is dead
The real tree has wilted, the pretty fairy too
Overwhelmingly bare, whatever will we do?

Don't be despondent, I have a good plan
Go to your local shop as quickly as you can
For Easter is around the corner, time to celebrate
Start buying chocolate eggs, don't leave it too late!

TO EAT OR NOT TO EAT

To eat or not to eat is always the question
I try to be good, avoid the acid indigestion
So why do I become weak when a chip shop is near
Failing to drive past as the fish supper leers?

The smell of the cod, the crunchiness of the batter
Oh, how I enjoy the temptation on the platter
A lashing of vinegar, a sprinkle of banned salt
It scares the statins, I've started my own revolt!

And what about the saveloy or posh sausage to me
Can bring mouth-watering pleasure, buy two get one free
Add a pickled egg and a dose of hot mushy peas
Not forgetting the beef burger, with onions and cheese!

A plateful of fat some people might want to question
Some might suggest, a cholesterol lesson
But then consider this a "good fat debate"
My mum ate pigs' trotters and lived to be eighty eight!

TO PEE OR NOT TO PEE

The cold feels nippier as I lie in my bed
My senses seem frozen as I lift my head
The warmth of the duvet falls short at my feet
Like a lamb in snow I am starting to bleat!

Whatever has happened, I feel so very wet
Surely incontinence has not soaked me yet
I suppose I must accept it with my advanced years
Hold back my concerns, stop the tears.

Buy some new knickers, plastic, discreet
Check the cushion before I leave the seat
But wait, it is okay, I now clearly see
It's water from the "hottie", not pee from me!

TOUGH LUCK

One person's happiness can mean sadness for another
Finding an empty toilet roll, when you've been to do the other
Or waving the family off on holiday, a trip to the sea
Only then, to realise, you're locked out without a key!

Or when you give your place up when standing in a queue
To be told when it's your turn "not letting any more through"
But despite this I remind myself, life is not always so cruel
Annoyingly to realise, my blooming car has run out of fuel!

DEAR LYN

I know you'll be surprised
Cos you didn't have a clue
That I would write a poem
Especially for you!

I don't want to upset you
But you really need to know
Those sweets you buy for singing
Clearly have to go!

They're not worth the money
The shop is conning you
Cos no matter how hard you suck
You still cough the whole way though!

Only Joking, Love You xxx

WHEN MAISIE CAME FOR TEA

When Maisie came for tea, she pushed in front of me
She wore an expressionless face, and sat down in my place!
My Mum didn't stop her; was too busy eating her roll
Well Maisie, she just smirked; her manners took their toll!

I would definitely take revenge, when we went outside to play
Something that I did, she remembers, to this day!
I took both of her plaits, and tied them to the fence
Along came next door's dog, I had my recompense!

The dog he was so friendly, he licked her face red raw
Maisie learnt some manners, something she lacked before!
I found it rather funny, my eyes leaked and leaked
I never noticed mum, when out the door she sneaked!

She lifted me by the scruff of my neck,
and pulled my trousers down
I wanted to die immediately; irritating Maisie won the crown!
What was Mum thinking of, embarrassing me this way?
Maisie had been so intolerable, what more was there to say?

Well, Mum, she had the last word,
As she smacked my backside raw
My face as red as Maisie's cheeks, my pride
sprawled on the floor!
"You mustn't treat our guest this way, it's a lesson learned
in life
Particularly not our Maisie, she's your future loving wife!"

WHEN YOU'RE GONE

So you think you'll last forever
And nothing will happen to you
Well that's what the Inca's thought
Before fifteen seventy-two

However, nothing lasts forever,
The Incas, once incredibly strong
Remain only as a testament
To when you're gone, you're gone!

So don't wait to wear purple
Or start that wishful bucket list
Do what you can while you're living
Because tomorrow might not exist!

This poem is not meant to be morbid
To scare, frighten or maim
It's written to gently reminder you
Like the Incas you'll never come again!

WHERE ART THOU VALENTINE

Oh! to have a Valentine, declaring their undying love
They say it's made in heaven, sent from God above
To have a bunch of flowers pressed firmly in my hand
Hear a card drop through the letterbox, oh so very grand!

To feel the pure excitement, smell the sweet aroma of his love
Two hearts fitting together, like a pair of rubber gloves
Someone to share my life with, make me a cup of tea
Filling my hot water bottle, cosy picnics by the sea.

Oh yes, if only I had a lover, my life would be complete
But, wait! I see a flower van, driving down my street
He's down my path, I'm beside myself,
And I have a lover for sure
"Sorry to bother you, love, can you take these, they're for her *next door!*"

WORRYING TO DEATH

I'm worried I won't find Heaven; my directional skills are
so poor
I'm worried I won't find Heaven, knock on the wrong blooming
door!
I'm worried I won't find Heaven; some say it's good for a rest
Others say they're not going, some say Earth is a test!
I am worried I won't find Heaven, so I am making sure I do
I am taking my "Satnav" with me; it's the sensible thing to do!

WORST NIGHTMARE

Have you ever woken up when not awake?
To find yourself eating, your favourite steak
On the very last bite, all covered in sauce
You open your eyes; wake up with a force!
You kick off the duvet, you're already late
You search the room, in a frenzied state
Disappointed and annoyed, it can't be true
Your worst nightmare, you've eaten your shoe!

YOU ARE WHAT YOU EAT

I was laying in bed, a fat lump of lard
My hair's turned pink, my body a façade!
I turned on the telly, I couldn't sleep
The programme pricked my conscience
"You are what you eat"
I couldn't believe it, I stared at the floor
A mountain of chocolate, blocking the door!
Shiny empty wrappers, once full of gelatine
The biggest pile of rubbish, ever to be seen!
"You are what you eat"
Please don't blame me, they entice me in
On special offer, I know they're a sin
I try to ignore them, hurry through the shop
They see me immediately... Stop! Stop! Stop!
"I am what I eat" not a pretty sight
Embarrassingly pink, I'm a Turkish Delight

LAUGHTER

Laughter is a therapy that enhances all you do
Exercises the face muscles, you feel younger too
Relieves the feelings of stress, stimulates your heart
The only downside is, it sometimes makes you fart!

THE LAST WORD

I just want to thank you for reading my book of poems, and if just one poem in this book strikes a chord with you and puts a smile on your face, then that makes me smile too.
Love from me to you xx

Also by Linda West

A poet who embraces a range of topics with gusto, a keen eye and a great dollop of humour.

www.ingramcontent.com/pod-product-compliance
Lightning Source LLC
LaVergne TN
LVHW010305070426
835507LV00027B/3446